Robert Sengstacke Abbott

A Man, a Paper, and a Parade

NICHOLS MIDDLE SCHOOL
800 GREENLEAF STREET
EVANSTON, IL 60202

Robert Sengstacke Abbott
A Man, a Paper, and a Parade

by Susan Engle

illustrated by Luthando Mazibuko

BELLWOOD
PRESS

WILMETTE, ILLINOIS

Bellwood Press, Wilmette, Illinois
401 Greenleaf Ave, Wilmette, Illinois 60091
Copyright © 2019 by the National Spiritual Assembly of
the Bahá'ís of the United States
All rights reserved. Published 2019
Printed in the United States of America ∞
24   23   22   21   4   3   2

Library of Congress Cataloging in Publication Data

Names: Engle, Susan, author.
Title: Robert Sengstacke Abbott : a man, a paper,
    and a parade / Susan Engle.
Description: Wilmette : Bellwood Press, 2019. |
    Includes bibliographical references.
Identifiers: LCCN 2018044247 | ISBN 9781618511355
    (softcover)
Subjects: LCSH: Abbott, Robert S. (Robert Sengstacke),
    1868–1940. | Journalists—United States—
    Biography. | African American journalist—
    United States—Biography. | Publishers and
    publishing—United States—Biography.
Classification: LCC PN4874.A235 E54 2019 |
    DDC 070.92 [B]—dc23
LC record available at https://lccn.loc.gov/2018044247

Cover art and illustrations by Luthando Mazibuko
Book design by Patrick Falso

To all people whose voices are not heard in our world

Contents

Acknowledgments

Giving life to the story of a person who is no longer living can be tricky. Mr. Abbott died nine years before I was born, so there was no opportunity for me to interview him, nor was there any film footage to review. After much reading and reflection—plus a trip to St. Simons Island, Georgia, the place where he was born—I began to form a picture of the man and his work, and I loved what I discovered about him. Perhaps he will someday be seen by many as the hero that he truly was.

This book would never have begun without the encouragement of Bonnie Taylor and her family. I also appreciated the assistance of my daughters, Bahiyyih Baker and Layli Phillips, who made excellent suggestions as the manuscript developed. Finally, I am grateful to Robert Sengstacke Abbott for leading such a noble and fulfilling life, which inspired this effort to make him real to generations of children who may know something about *The Chicago Defender* and Bud Billiken, but nothing about the man who started a paper and a parade.

Introduction

Waiting for a hungry fish to grab the hook disguised with a big fat worm, a young boy sat under a tree by the Savannah River. He'd had enough of people this sunny afternoon and was happy to be by himself. Usually he didn't let the teasing from schoolmates and his brothers and

sisters or bullying from white people—and from people whose skin was somewhere between his rich, dark, chocolate skin and white skin—bother him too much. Things were the way they were.[1]

In the murmuring water, he felt as if he heard his stepfather's voice, telling him about his family, as he did so often. "You have a proud heritage, child. Your father was of the Igbo people of Western Africa. One of the sailing ships holding his kidnapped relatives being brought to slavery anchored off the coast of Georgia's very own St. Simon's Island, where you were born. A group of the bravest, singing, jumped into the water. They drowned because they were not willing to spend the rest of their lives being treated with the deep disrespect and cruelty they had experienced in the weeks of their terrible voyage to America."[2]

The splash of a frog jumping in the water startled the child back to his fishing line. He checked the hook and saw that half of the worm had been nibbled away. Oh well. Half a worm could work. The day was so warm. He wouldn't think about that ship today—not the way he did sometimes in the middle of the night. He settled back and let the words continue.

"Your mother's people were stolen from Portuguese West Africa. When they arrived here, her father became a skilled craftsman—a painter and decorator—for his slave master. Her mother had to be a Mammy and run a whole household, which included bringing up the children of the white man's family. At the same time, she raised six children of her own. When her first daughter, your mother Flora, grew old enough, she became a nursemaid for this family. Flora longed to read and write, so in the early mornings before her work began, she secretly taught herself by making a rubbing, with tissue paper and a pencil, of the letters on the brass name-plates next to her neighbors' doors. Have I told you that before? If anyone had discovered what she was doing, she would have been severely punished. She is brave—and practical—your mother."[3]

The high buzz of a sparrow's song above his head jerked him back. Looking at the empty hook, the child sighed and threaded a new wiggling worm a little more carefully. He watched the line, but his papa's voice bubbled on.

"And just like you, even though we are not blood relatives, I know the prejudice in this country where we live. My father was a German sea captain. When he traveled to Savannah, he decided to make his home here. One night, he found himself near a slave auction down by the piers. He had never experienced such a thing in Germany, so he quietly watched and listened to the sad sight—the loud auctioneers and sounds of grief coming from people being roughly inspected by buyers. He saw one young woman with tears streaming down her face. Her name was Tama. He suddenly realized he could save her from being a slave if he bought her. So he gave the auctioneers the price they insisted on and took her to South Carolina to marry her. It was illegal to marry here in Savannah. That is how Tama became my mother."4

"Since my skin is fairly light, I could pass as white. But when it was discovered that my mother was African, I was fired from my work as a translator and a teacher for white children. And now, as you know so well, I am a minister and a teacher in my own small school for black children."5

The quick pull of a fish! The voice in his head evaporated. This wiggler was putting up quite a fight. But the child knew from experience that he could land it and bring it back home for dinner.

He was proud to be who he was. And on that day, as well as many days and years afterward, he felt in his heart that he would do something to bring equality to this country. He would shout out the pain of prejudice and make his stepfather's motto above the door of his parsonage come true: "Overcome Evil with Good."[6]

1. A Difficult Beginning

On Thanksgiving Day in the year 1868, a baby was born on St. Simons Island. In a cabin surrounded by oak trees trailing long strands of Spanish moss, Flora Abbott went through the labor and birth of her son. She was all alone. No doctors or family attended to her pain or the child being born. She named her baby Robert and took care of him with all of her heart and strength. About a year before, she had lost a baby girl. She wanted this baby to live to grow up.[7]

Life was not easy for them. When Robert was four months old, his father, Thomas, died of tuberculosis. Though Thomas's sisters wanted to raise baby Robert themselves, Flora took her child to the city of Savannah, about eighty miles away, to live with her mother.[8]

The Civil War had ended a few years ago, and now that Flora was a free woman, she could use her reading skills openly. She began to help her landlord, John H. H. Sengstacke, tutor young students.[9]

John helped Flora when her former sisters-in-law tried to take Robert away from her. He hired a lawyer to defend her in court, and in the end, Flora was allowed to keep her baby. She was grateful for this help and later wrote of John, "We became fond of each other and decided to marry." And they did marry on July 26, 1874, when Robert was five years old.[10]

Two years later, John became a minister with a church and started a school in the small city of Woodville near Savannah. He formally adopted seven-year-old Robert, and Robert Abbott became Robert Sengstacke.[11]

2. Happy Days

Robert was the first of eight children, the rest of whom would be born over the years in the new family. For five months of the year, they all attended their father's school. On days when there was no school, they played and hunted in the woods and fished in the river nearby.[12]

The children also had work to do for the family. Robert took care of the horses and planted corn and potatoes. He loved horses and was able to harness one him-

self, even in the dark stable in the early mornings.[13]

At the end of each day, the large family gathered around a potbellied stove, lit the lanterns, talked, and listened to "Papa" Sengstacke read from the Bible. Often, they would end up singing together.[14]

Singing was also part of the entertainment called a "shout" in their community, a tradition that had come with the people from West Africa. Friends would gather in a home, push back all the furniture, and form a circle. A leader would start a song and direct different voices to join in. Clapping and stomping kept the rhythm. Robert, with his clear tenor voice, was eager to join in.[15]

When Robert was little, Reverend John Sengstacke would carry him on his shoulders during their many walks together. Reverend Sengstacke took his work as a helper to his churchgoers—as well as all the African-American people in the surrounding countryside—very seriously. During these walks, he often stopped to

teach poor farmers certain skills, such as how to grow fruits and vegetables—including cucumbers, English peas, and strawberries, all of which were hard to get. Then the fruits and vegetables could be sold in Savannah. He also gave the farmers tips for basic hygiene, such as not sharing a toothbrush with six other people. Robert's father cared about justice as much as education. He took Robert to sessions at a courthouse to watch cases being tried. If an African-American defendant was not being treated fairly, John would ask to speak up for him in court.[16]

It was on these walks that John would talk to his son about the teasing and bullying he was facing from people because of his skin color. In the United States, white skin meant a person had power and authority. To most Americans, black skin meant someone was less intelligent, less talented, less valuable. John wanted the best for his children, and he wanted for them to be able to see themselves for the good people they were, no matter what others said or thought.[17]

In the end, the bullying Robert faced may have added to his determination—some might say stubbornness—whenever he was faced with a challenge. His step-father's encouragement on their walks showed Robert that, no matter how other people treated him on account of his dark skin, he could help his own people find justice and equality in a land that had yet to live up to its name, "the land of the free."

During the summers, as he grew older, Robert would do odd jobs, sometimes as an errand boy, in nearby Savannah. As part of his practical education, his mother insisted that Robert give her money from his earnings to pay for his room, his food, and his laundry. As much as Robert loved riding horses and singing at home, when he was in the city, he enjoyed watching the Georgia Cadets parading in the streets. During the years of Jim Crow laws that followed the end of slavery, many activities in the black community were declared illegal, and these groups of marching military African-American teenagers would eventually be outlawed. But Robert's attraction to their skill planted a respect for the military in his heart that lasted for the rest of his life.[18]

3. What Shall I Do?

Robert Sengstacke wanted to succeed. And his stepfather wanted all of his eight children to have a college education. But Reverend Sengstacke despaired of his ability, as a poor teacher and minister, to send them away to school. With some effort, the reverend found people who supported his church and who came to his aid. As a result of their assistance, Robert, his oldest, was able to attend two schools to get him ready to enter college.[19]

Robert was not certain about which career he would choose. He did not want to become a minister because he was unhappy that churches did not accept all people in their congregations. Each church allowed only people with one particular color of skin to become members and worship together. He had also thought about becoming a teacher, but he was not sure he could truly change prejudice against black people in the whole country by teaching a few students in a classroom every year. There *was* something that appealed to him, however, and that was the printed word. He often thought about becoming a publisher of newspapers, magazines, and books. So, determined to study the printing process, he started his first year in a university in 1889 when he was twenty-one years old.[20]

Robert traveled almost five hundred miles, most likely by train, which would have taken more than a day, to reach his new school in Hampton, Virginia. He must have been happy to finally arrive at Hampton University, a trade and agricultural school with ivy-covered buildings set among oak trees. However, Robert was not terribly happy there when classes started. Perhaps because he felt like a fish out of water in his new environment, Robert adopted an aggressive and pushy attitude toward his fellow students. His classmates, for their part, were quick to pick up on his sensitivity to his dark skin, and they teased him constantly about it.

The chaplain at Hampton, Dr. Frissell, noticed Robert was having difficulties. One night, he visited a sad Robert alone in his room. He asked about Robert's feelings and discovered that the young man was discouraged by the continuing prejudice he felt at Hampton. With a kind and friendly manner, Dr. Frissell suggested that Robert would probably face discrimination all his life in the United States. Perhaps he could be of service in the world by finding a way to show black and white people that we are all one human family. This idea, spoken by someone who would become and remain one of Robert's most loyal friends, sounded like the advice of his much-loved stepfather, and Robert took it to heart. He later wrote that he now became known as "Happy Bob" on campus.[21]

An unexpected career path opened up to him during his Hampton years. Robert's beautiful tenor voice was heard at a gathering in the church on campus, and he was invited to join a musical group called the Hampton Quartet. This led to some of his happiest moments in college. He loved singing with these fellow students, and he also loved traveling around the country, which the Hampton Quartet did regularly to help raise money for the school. One of the quartet's trips took him to New York, where the four men performed for a famous conductor and composer. After hearing him sing, Walter Damrosch offered Robert a scholarship to the Institute of Musical Art in New York City—later known as Juilliard School—that Mr. Damrosch's brother, Frank, had founded. But Robert was discouraged from accepting the offer by Dr. Frissell, who was traveling with the quartet. Dr. Frissell thought that the time was not ripe for a black man to make a living in music, and he felt that although music was one of Robert's talents, it was probably not the one that would help him become most successful in this country at this time in its history.[22]

Another one of these trips took him to Chicago, where he had the joy of hearing Frederick Douglass, a former enslaved man and an excellent orator, speak about the equality of black and white people at

the World's Fair in Chicago in 1893. Confirming his idea that all people deserved to be treated equally, Robert watched this black man win the respect of a largely white audience, and it filled him with hope. He also met the fearless journalist Ida B. Wells. She and Mr. Douglass had worked on a pamphlet for the Fair that outlined the evils of lynching and segregation in the United States. The defiant writing would have an influence on Robert's future work in the newspaper business.[23]

By 1896, Robert had finished his schooling at Hampton University. He still was not completely certain about what to do next, so he returned home to help his father publish a local newspaper and teach school. While there, he fell in love with the beautiful young Catherine Scarborough, the daughter of one of his stepfather's friends. Catherine was mulatto, however, and her family thought that a man with dark skin was not good enough for their daughter. When Catherine accepted a watch with Robert's picture inside, Robert asked her to marry him. Regardless of how she may have felt about Robert personally, Catherine listened to her parents and rejected the offer from this very dark man with little money.[24]

The rejection hurt Robert deeply. Now doubly determined to succeed in a career that would enable him to earn an income acceptable to a future wife, Robert moved to Chicago and became a student at Kent College of Law. When he registered for school, he used the name Robert Sengstacke Abbott for the first time, claiming his natural father's name from then on until the end of his life. Nearly penniless, he worked during the day and went to school at night. He even took the time to form a drill corps of African-American boys in his neighborhood to help keep them occupied with something besides the life of the streets. Robert graduated in 1899 with a Bachelor of Law degree—the only black student in his class.[25]

Once again, however, his color got in the way of his hopes for his future. Though he made several attempts to work as a lawyer in Kansas and Illinois, he saw that the majority of African Americans could not afford to hire him. And white people were not interested in black attorneys. A fellow African-American lawyer told him that he was "a little too dark to make an impression on the courts of Chicago."[26]

In 1904, his beloved stepfather died. Robert quickly made two decisions. To honor the man who had raised him, he started raising money from white people who would support a school for African-American children in Georgia. He planned to build a school that would carry his stepfather's name, and for a short time, he began leaning toward a career in education. But living in the South again seemed guaranteed to keep him away from becoming successful. Slavery had ended, but the blatant prejudice shown against black Americans in the South was a powerful reason to leave. Suddenly, to his family's surprise, he decided he needed to start a newspaper in Chicago. Maybe he was hearing his stepfather's words in his head: "A good newspaper was one of the best instruments of service and one of the strongest weapons ever to be used in defense of a race which was deprived of its citizenship rights."

Publishing a newspaper, more than any career he had considered, might give him a chance to change the world.[27]

4. A Twenty-Five Cent Start

Publishing a newspaper was not new to Robert. After all, he had studied printing at Hampton University and had worked on a newspaper as a summer job. He had

also helped his stepfather's paper, the *Woodville Times*. Now, he felt he was ready to begin on his own. For the first step, he rented a room for an office with a single card table and a typewriter. For the second step, he used the 25 cents in his pocket—enough money for two sandwiches and a cup of coffee—for paper and pencils.[28]

At age 37, he had found the place to put all his energy. And he would need it. He was his own reporter and newsboy, as well as his own editor and all of the newspaper jobs in between. Friends helped him come up with a name. Someone suggested "The Defender," and Robert added

"Chicago." Indeed, *The Chicago Defender* would begin by printing news of Robert's neighbors in the city. Little did he know at the time that his paper would grow to print over 200,000 copies per issue, would be distributed across the United States, and would turn him into a millionaire.[29]

Robert spent a lot of time talking to people he met on the street. He was very good at putting humorous stories together for people's entertainment from news he heard. One local item in 1905, the first year of *The Chicago Defender,* was called "Polly Took Her Vacation." It described the day a parrot took off from the window of her owner's home, squawking about the heat in the kitchen: "Give me a fan, woman!" It returned nearly a week later with another squawk about the high temperatures in Chicago.[30]

Other articles dealt with the talks of prominent African Americans and visitors from Africa to Chicago—news that the other papers of the city did not cover. But within a few years, *The Defender* began to report on the injustices being suffered by black people in America and began living up to its slogan: "American Race Prejudice must be destroyed." Stories of African Americans being killed by mobs and the Ku Klux Klan in the South were reported, as well as other grave injustices. The majority of these crimes were never brought to court. And if they were, the white people charged with the crimes were not found guilty.[31]

Even though he had only enough money for a place to stay and a meal or two every day, Robert kept going. Somehow he juggled the debts he had to print the paper with the small amounts that came in from selling the paper on the street. Slowly, his fortunes began to change. By 1915, *The Chicago Defender* was the most widely read black newspaper in the United States. For Robert, the paper's growth was more than a personal success. It was a step forward for the United States. As he printed in the paper in 1916, "With drops of ink, we make people think!"[32]

5. African Americans on the Move

Robert Abbott would never forget how he and people of his race were treated in the South. He had moved to Chicago to escape the worst of the Jim Crow laws—having to use restrooms and drinking fountains separate from whites; being required to move off the sidewalk whenever a white person approached; having to listen to grown men with no recourse being called "boy" and other negative words by white men, women, and children; and being unable to find homes outside of restricted areas or work at jobs with a decent living wage. Robert wanted other black Americans to experience some of the small freedoms that living in the North could bring, especially better pay for work. Another example of this kind of freedom was a growing section of Chicago that was filled with businesses that understood and catered to the tastes and habits of African Americans.[33]

In his paper, Robert began to publish more firsthand accounts of mistreatment by white people in the South. By publishing ads for apartments that could be rented and work that could be found, he encouraged his people to leave and find a better life in Chicago. He was so successful that *The Defender* became one of the chief instruments for inspiring hundreds of thousands of African Americans to begin what is now called the Great Migration—the movement of large numbers of black families to the northern and western United States.[34]

White businessmen and farmers in the South grew alarmed. They were beginning to lose more and more of the inexpensive labor on which they had depended for centuries. As a result, *The Chicago Defender* became outlawed in some Southern towns. If people were caught distributing it, they could be forced to leave their homes, be beaten, or even killed.[35]

To get around the problem of getting the paper safely to people in the South, *The Defender* was partly distributed by black musicians and entertainers who could drive into town and drop the paper off without being caught. African-American Pullman porters on trains threw bundles of papers out in prearranged spots for others to pick up and distribute. Every issue was passed around and read by entire church congregations and neighborhoods.[36]

6. A Dangerous Business

Now that the paper was becoming more widespread and influential, Robert began to receive death threats.[37] Some people let him know that they would shut down his paper and kill him if they could. In one incident, a small town in Georgia sent a Sheriff Moon to the *Defender* offices in Chicago. It seems that the paper had caused a stir by reporting the disrespectful words of a racist judge running for reelection.

The sheriff burst into Robert's office, not knowing which person was the newspaper owner. Robert told him to return later in the afternoon and recruited a friend, Dr. George C. Hall, to stand in for

him. When the sheriff returned, Dr. Hall was in the office chair, posing as Robert.

"Is this Abbott?" Sheriff Moon demanded.

"*Mister* Abbott," Dr. Hall corrected.

Less aggressively now, the sheriff replied, "I've come to take Mr. Abbott back with me."

"Where's your [legal] papers?" Dr. Hall demanded.

The sheriff handed them over. After reading them carefully, Dr. Hall tore them up into little pieces and threw them into the trash. "Don't you know this is Illinois—not Georgia! You can't get away with that in this town!"

Quickly, Sheriff Moon left the office and did not return.[38]

Robert Abbott, though criticized from many quarters, survived without being killed or imprisoned by the people who hated his newspaper and its insistence on equal treatment. In big and small ways, he continued to work to urge white and black people to think about the truth of every situation. For instance, from the end of the 1800s, amusement parks across the country featured a game called "African Dodger." A black man would make himself a target for wooden balls that were thrown at his head. If a carnival customer succeeded in hitting him, the winning pitcher was awarded a cigar. *The Defender* tried to get the game stopped, but it was too good a moneymaker for parks to agree to end it. Then the paper appealed to black people to stop allowing themselves to be the targets, even if it meant sacrificing the meager pay. The game disappeared during Robert's lifetime.[39]

In every paper, Robert chose to focus on issues of racial prejudice and defended African Americans who were targeted for injustice in America. During World War II, he published stories of black service-men who were segregated from whites and were treated with disrespect. Stories were printed that exposed facts about lynchings and "riots" where black men were killed and no one brought to court to pay for the murders. The paper objected to the showing of a film with scenes celebrating the Ku Klux Klan in a positive light and showing a fictional black man threatening a white child. This film, *The Birth of a Nation*, was shown in Chicago in spite of the paper's objections.[40]

In every instance, *The Chicago Defender* published news from the point of view of the African-American men, women, and children who were being misrepresented in white newspapers. By this time, Robert knew that he would be risking assassination if he traveled to the South, but his newspaper continued to give black people a voice in the press.

7. His Proudest Possession

The Chicago Defender kept getting bigger and better. By 1919, Robert had purchased his own printing press, and by 1920, the paper had grown to employ sixty-eight people to do the work he had accomplished by himself when the paper started. *The Defender* was able to print stories about the achievements of black people, as well as stories of injustices they suffered, because Robert wanted to encourage the hearts of African Americans as well as entertain and educate them. To

make the paper livelier, comic strips were added, along with sections especially for women.[41]

But it was not until 1921 that Robert Abbott added a page just for kids called "Defender Junior." His biographer, Roi

Ottley, wrote that this kids' section, which featured a fictional kid editor named Bud Billiken, eventually "developed into a gigantic project that involved more than a quarter million participants" and was Robert Abbott's "proudest possession." Bud Billiken was a name made up from little good luck dolls, called billikens, that cost a quarter and were popular at the time. Robert was especially fond of the Bud Billiken idea because he could follow in his stepfather's footsteps by encouraging children to become excellent readers. He also hoped to give moral role models to children in the articles and stories that were chosen for their pages.[42]

Not only could kids read letters and an editorial created just for them, they could also have articles published in the "Defender Junior" pages about their parties and accomplishments. Just as exciting, they could join the Bud Billiken Club. Since black kids were barred from joining white Boy Scout troops at the time, becoming a Bud Billiken Club member was a way to give African-American kids an organization that made them proud to be themselves. And once they were members, they received a personalized membership card and a special identification button.[43]

Two young boys are credited with being the fictional editor Bud Billiken at different times. One was Willard Motley, who had sent a story to *The Defender* when he was thirteen years old. He wrote to the kids, "Before I came here I used to come home in the afternoon and write. Now I come to *The Defender* office and see how many of you have written to me." He grew up to write a bestselling novel called *Knock on Any Door.*[44]

The other young editor was ten years old when he wrote a column as Bud Biliken and read the hundreds of letters that poured in from kids. Robert Watkins was chosen from among the newsboys who came to the office to pick up copies of the paper to sell. He was described as "a quiet, sad-eyed, soft-spoken and well-mannered little fellow." Since he was so young, he had to get his mother's permission to take his seat at a desk in the paper's headquarters after school.[45]

In his first column as editor, Robert Watkins introduced himself. He wrote, "Now I am just *breaking in* on this newspaper game, and you will have to help me out. I am not like other people on this paper who think they know everything. Billiken is my name. They call me 'Bud' for short. I am not kin to the little fellow they sell in stores for 25 cents; I'm better lookin' than he is, and I got more *sense*. What I want to say is this. Mr. Abbott and those other editors here are giving me a chance to earn some popcorn money. They want me to fill in this column with sayings and doings of we little folks." He continued as editor until he entered high school.[46]

In time, Robert Abbott and one of his employees, David W. Kellum, developed a new way to reward Bud Billiken Club members and the newsboys who sold *The Defender* on the street. First, in 1924, they held a big party, a picnic. By 1929, the party had turned into a parade. In 1930, the second Bud Billiken parade was held in Chicago in February. It was zero degrees that day! Nevertheless, the parade rolled through the frozen streets with a few hardy onlookers. It ended at the Royal Theater with a day of free candy; competitions, such as a greasy pole-climbing and a shoe-tying contest; a crowning of young kings—kids who sold the most subscriptions during the year; a movie; a professional clown; and a concert with the famed Louis Armstrong.[47]

Thereafter, the annual parade was moved to a warmer time in Chicago, and on every second Saturday in August, kids get ready for the Bud Billiken Parade by competing to win scholarships and become parade royalty. Famous celebrities and politicians ride in the parade every year and have included Chance the Rapper, Oprah Winfrey, boxer Muhammad Ali, and Senator Barack Obama and his wife, Michelle. Marching bands and drill teams accompany the floats and celebrities, and the parade always ends with a gathering in Washington Park for food, face painting, and gifts of school supplies. The Bud Billiken Parade, a celebration of African-American community and heritage, is the second largest parade in the United States—second only to the Rose Bowl Parade in Pasadena, California.[48]

8. Search for a Church

Though sometimes described as a workaholic, Robert had a life outside of the newspaper. As he grew wealthier, he worked at being a role model for the African-American community by joining museums and attending opera and other musical events. He felt that God and religion were central to a successful and happy family, and he longed to find a church that fit his ideas of justice and equality. But this was not easy to do.[49]

Because his stepfather was a clergy-man, every Sunday of Robert's child-hood was devoted to the Congregational Church. The people who attended this church were all African Americans. None of them would have been welcome in the churches where white people worshipped. There were also churches in which only mulattos could be part of the congrega-tion. This separation of worshipers by skin color had always bothered Robert. He felt in his own mind that God did not sepa-rate people in this way in heaven. Surely it was only the purity of a person's soul that mattered to God. "Isn't that what should matter to all Christians?" Robert thought. "Shouldn't it matter to all people of any religion?"[50]

After Robert had moved to Chicago and started *The Defender*, he decided to go to an event at Hull House in Chicago during the spring of 1912. He thought that he would attend only to report on the meeting for the newspaper, but something about this speaker and his subject touched his heart.[51]

Hull House was a group of buildings in Chicago that was used to give immigrants a place to live and an opportunity to learn about their new country.[52] The social reformers who ran the settlement would often hold events that would have been of interest to the readers of *The Chicago Defender.*

This particular meeting was attended by around 750 people from various cultures. It was a talk given by a spiritual leader of the time about the equality of all people in the sight of God.[53] The leader's name was 'Abdu'l-Bahá, and he was the son of the Founder of the Bahá'í Faith, Bahá'u'lláh, Who had died twenty years earlier in the Holy Land in Palestine, the country known today as Israel.

'Abdu'l-Bahá was on a journey to Europe and America to tell people about

Bahá'u'lláh's teachings. The most important of these was the unity of people
everywhere, regardless of their wealth or
poverty, their nationality, race, or their
religion. This was a message Robert Abbott
could agree with one hundred percent.

Part of Robert's account of this meeting was published in *The Defender* on May
4, 1912:

> The reception at Hull House
> was a very delightful and interesting
> affair. That wonderful teacher of
> peace and the brotherhood of man,
> 'Abdu'l-Bahá, of Persia, made his
> first appearance at the Hull House.

In both of his addresses at Hull House and Handel hall, 'Abdu'l-Bahá very eloquently showed the folly of discrimination on the account of the only point of difference between men, that of the color of the skin.

A garden of flowers, all of one color, would be monotonous and by no means beautiful.[54]

When the talk ended, Robert approached the speaker at the podium, who put a hand on Robert's head. 'Abdu'l-Bahá told him that he would be of service to humanity. Robert never forgot this experience.

He reported stories about the Bahá'í Faith in several editions of *The Chicago Defender* as the years passed, and he began to read Bahá'í books.[55]

Meanwhile, Robert was worshipping at an Episcopal church. Then he attended a Presbyterian church in Chicago. No matter which congregation he joined, however, people made him feel unwelcome because of his dark skin. He even volunteered to use his beautiful tenor voice in a church choir, but he was rejected. Eventually he turned to Christian Science. But in time, when white people and black people were required to worship separately, he left the religion.[56]

Finally, he attended a gathering in Wilmette, Illinois, on June 3, 1934. It was the annual National Convention of the Bahá'ís of the United States being held in the lower level of the Bahá'í House of Worship. In the meeting, the Bahá'ís were speaking about the positive public-

ity that the Bahá'í Faith had received in *The Chicago Defender*. A voice spoke up in the audience: "Dr. Abbott is now here with us." He was then asked to address the crowd, and these are his words:

> Dear friends . . . Happy am I to see people whom I have been praying to God all my life to see, those who recognize me as a man. Everywhere I have travelled I have been received as a man save in my own country. Here my people have been cruelly treated and even burned at the stake! . . . 'Abdu'l-Bahá when in America put His hand on my

head and told me that He would get from me some day a service for the benefit of Humanity. I am identifying myself with this Cause and I go up with you or down with you. Anything for this Cause! Let it go out and remove the darkness everywhere. Save my people! Save America from herself![57]

Robert Sengstacke Abbott had found a religion of equality, a religion that embraced him exactly as he was.

9. Courageous Defender

After his stepfather's death in 1904, Robert not only became a defender of millions of his fellow African Americans through his paper, he also took on the responsibility of his stepfather's dream: that all of his children should become educated. Over the years, when *The Defender* earned enough money, Robert paid for the schooling of all ten of his nieces and nephews. He even carried that responsibility over the Atlantic Ocean to the children of his stepfather's family and provided education for three German relatives.[58]

Perhaps the most surprising help he gave was to a white family in the South. The Stevens family had owned a plantation on St. Simons Island, Georgia, and were the owners of enslaved people. One of them was Robert's father, Thomas Abbott. During the Depression, they must have known about Robert's success in Chicago. They asked him for financial assistance, and he sent them money for six years.[59]

What could have inspired them to reach out to Robert? It could have been that his father had been a trustworthy person. When the Civil War began and the Stevens family left their plantation to wait out the war, Thomas took action. He moved all the silver from the house and hid it. Then, he had the other slaves take all of the valuable furniture to the slave quarters. He figured that the invading army would never imagine such beautiful pieces would be found there, and he was right. When the Stevens family returned after the war was over, all the silver had been polished, and all the furniture was returned to the plantation home unharmed by the soldiers![60]

And what could have inspired Robert to help the people who had enslaved his father? Maybe it was that Robert wanted to keep his father's good reputation alive. Or maybe it was that Robert wished to show others what he believed—that no matter what color a person's skin might be, all people are deserving of kindness and equality.

It was only six years after his commitment to the Bahá'í Faith that Robert Sengstacke Abbott lost his life to Bright's disease, a problem fatally affecting his kidneys. He died in his sleep on Thursday, February 29, 1940.[61] He was seventy-one years old.

On the following Monday in Chicago, he was treated as a hero of the American people. Flags flew at half-mast, and the

Chicago Defender building was draped in black. Thousands gathered to hear the funeral service played over loudspeakers that had been set up near the Metropolitan Community Church. Messages and tributes that came in—from a Boy Scout troop named after him all the way to the mayor of Chicago—were printed for everyone to read. A caravan of African-American policemen and firemen led the funeral procession along the same route that Robert's much-loved Bud Billiken parade had taken every year.

Thousands bowed their heads for the procession to the cemetery. More than 250 cars filled with family and dignitaries made the journey to his burial. During the graveside service, two airplanes flew in low and dropped six American Beauty roses from above onto the grave of the man who had served his people so well.

Lucius Harper, who helped create the Bud Billiken character with Robert and who became the executive editor of *The Chicago Defender,* wrote on the front page of the paper that week:

The Dean of Negro journalism is dead . . . He educated his race to demand their rights as men. He brought them out of the swamps of shackles and discouragement into the promised land of hope and liberty. The South despised him for his courage, and with death threats forbade him to return to the land of his birth. He knew no defeat. . . .

His early life as a journalist and abolitionist against wrong was one of toil, poverty and hardship . . . He never lost the common touch; he was a militant defender of the lowly. He believed in his race and in God.

Lucky are the sons of black men when such martyrs and faithful servants to a race as Robert S. Abbott are born upon earth.

Above their neglected cradles sing the morning stars and around their humble homes, hushed and expectant, await the early breezes that shall drive away the fog and mist before the rising sun so a race of men, bruised by shackles, can see clear to progress and achieve.

Farewell, Chief, you have pointed to a star . . . may it give light to our weary feet along the pathway to hope . . .[62]

Arriving in Chicago today, you can drive by Robert Sengstacke Abbott's house, a National Historic Landmark since 1976.

You can visit his gravesite in the Lincoln
Cemetery in nearby Alsip, Illinois, where
his headstone shows a torch engraved with
the words *knowledge, truth, and enlighten-*

ment. And if you should happen to plan a trip to Chicago on the second Saturday in August, you can watch the Bud Billiken parade and enjoy a day of celebration of the African Americans who contribute so much to this country. If Robert were still here to greet you, you might just see him smile.

Timeline

Important Events in the Life of
Robert Sengstacke Abbott

1868 Born on St. Simons Island, Georgia, on Thanksgiving Day.*

1869 Robert's father, Thomas, dies of tuberculosis.

1874 Flora, Robert's mother, marries John H. H. Sengstacke.

1876 The newly ordained John adopts Robert.

1889 Starts college at Hampton University to study printing.

1892 Is offered a music scholarship at Juilliard School, but turns it down.

1893 Hears Frederick Douglass speak at the World Columbian Exhibition in Chicago.

1896 Graduates from Hampton University.

1897 Begins school at Kent College of Law.

1899 Earns a Bachelor of Law degree.

1904 Attends funeral of beloved stepfather.

1905	Publishes the first issue of *The Chicago Defender*.
1917	Motivates African Americans to move out of the South, starting the "Great Migration."
1919	Circulation of *The Chicago Defender* reaches 230,000.
1921	Begins "Defender Junior" section with young editor "Bud Billiken."
1929	First Bud Billiken parade.
1934	Announces publicly his membership in the Bahá'í Faith.
1939	Hands control of the *Defender* to his nephew, John H. Sengstacke III.
1940	Breathes his last breath in his sleep.

* In a footnote on page 24 of Abbott's biography, Roi Ottley writes: "Robert S. Abbott believed he was born November 24, 1870, but the Parish Register (1868–1900) of St. Stephens Episcopal Church (now St. Matthews), Savannah, where he was baptized, records his birth at the above date." Even his headstone reads "1870."

Notes

1. Michaeli, *The Defender: How the Legendary Black Newspaper Changed America*, pp. 7–8; Ottley, *The Lonely Warrior*, p. 13.
2. Ottley, *The Lonely Warrior*, p. 20.
3. Ibid., pp. 25, 26.
4. Ibid., p. 29.
5. Ibid., p. 33.
6. Ibid., p. 42.
7. Ibid., pp. 23–24.
8. Ibid., pp. 26–27.
9. Michaeli, *The Defender: How the Legendary Black Newspaper Changed America*, p. 6.
10. Ottley, *The Lonely Warrior*, p. 27; Michaeli, *The Defender: How the Legendary Black Newspaper Changed America*, p. 6; Ottley, *The Lonely Warrior*, p. 36.
11. Michaeli, *The Defender: How the Legendary Black Newspaper Changed America*, p. 6; Ottley, *The Lonely Warrior*, p. 37.

12. "Robert S. Abbott," at the Notable Names Database (NNDB), http://www.nndb.com/people/733/000141310/; Michaeli, *The Defender: How the Legendary Black Newspaper Changed America*, p. 6; Ottley, *The Lonely Warrior*, p. 38.

13. Ottley, *The Lonely Warrior*, pp. 43–44.

14. Ibid., p. 44.

15. Ibid., p. 39.

16. Ibid., pp. 48, 52–53.

17. Michaeli, *The Defender: How the Legendary Black Newspaper Changed America*, pp. 7–8.

18. Ottley, *The Lonely Warrior*, p. 44; Michaeli, *The Defender: How the Legendary Black Newspaper Changed America*, p. 7.

19. Ottley, *The Lonely Warrior*, pp. 46–47, 62–63.

20. Ibid., pp. 35–36, 66–67.

21. Ibid., pp. 68–70.

22. Ibid., pp. 70–72; Michaeli, *The Defender: How the Legendary Black Newspaper Changed America*, p. 9.

23. Ottley, *The Lonely Warrior*, p. 74; Michaeli, *The Defender: How the Legendary Black Newspaper Changed America*, p. 14.

24. Ottley, *The Lonely Warrior*, pp. 73, 74–76.

25. Ibid., p. 77.

26. Ibid., pp. 77–78.

27. Ibid., pp. 78–80, 1.

28. Ibid., pp. 44, 74–75, 87; Whitaker, Jan. "What Would a Nickel Buy?" *Restaurant-ing Through History,* https://restaurant-ingthroughhistory. com/2013/07/31/what-would-a-nickel-buy/.

29. Michaeli, *The Defender: How the Legendary Black Newspaper Changed America,* p. 20; Ottley, *The Lonely Warrior,* pp. 87, 200; according to the National Names Database, ". . . the *Defender* had half a million readers at its peak," http://www.nndb. com/people/733/000141310/; "Robert S. Abbott," the National Names Database, http://www.nndb. com/people/733/000141310/; Michaeli, *The Defender: How the Legendary Black Newspaper Changed America,* p. 166; Ottley, *The Lonely Warrior,* p. 1.

30. Ottley, *The Lonely Warrior,* pp. 88, 93, 91.

31. DeSantis, "A Forgotten Leader Robert S. Abbott and the Chicago Defender from 1910–1920," p. 2, 56, https://www.questia.com/library/ journal/1P3-185333497/a-forgotten-leader-robert-s-abbott-and-the-chicago; DeSantis, "A Forgotten Leader Robert S. Abbott and the Chicago Defender from 1910–1920," p. 9, http://shmacek. faculty.noctrl.edu/Courses/ChicagoMedia/ AbbottandChicagoDef.pdf; "Robert S. Abbott," the National Names Database, http://www.nndb. com/people/733/000141310/.

32. Michaeli, *The Defender: How the Legendary Black Newspaper Changed America*, pp. 23–25; Whitmore, *The Inspirational Life of Robert Sengstacke Abbott,* p. 7, http://www.theabbottinstitute.org/assets/abbott_brucewhitmore_thelifeofrobertsengstackeabbott.pdf; Ottley, *The Lonely Warrior*, p. 121.

33. American Public Radio, Part One. "Remembering Jim Crow," http://americanradioworks.publicradio.org/features/remembering/transcript.html; Ottley, *The Lonely Warrior*, pp. 81–82; WTTW, "DuSable to Obama: Chicago's Black Metropolis," p. 1, https://interactive.wttw.com/dusable-to-obama/black-business.

34. Grossman, "The Great Migration: For southern blacks, Chicago offered jobs—but not the warmest welcome from whites," p. 1, http://www.chicagotribune.com/news/opinion/commentary/ct-perspec-flash-great-migration-south-african-americans-0415-20180410-story.html; Ottley, *The Lonely Warrior,* pp. 160–61.

35. Wallace, "Chicago Defender," p. 1, http://www.encyclopedia.chicagohistory.org/pages/248.html; DeSantis, "A Forgotten Leader Robert S. Abbott and the Chicago Defender from 1910–1920," p. 7, http://shmacek.faculty.noctrl.edu/Courses/ChicagoMedia/AbbottandChicagoDef.pdf.

36. "Founder Editor—Robert S. Abbott," graph 3, https://www.pbs.org/blackpress/news_bios/defender.html.

37. Ottley, *The Lonely Warrior*, pp. 146 and 149; Whitmore, *The Inspirational Life of Robert Sengstacke Abbott*, p. 11, http://www.theabbottinstitute.org/assets/abbott_brucewhitmore_thelifeofrobertsengstackeabbott.pdf.

38. Ottley, *The Lonely Warrior*, pp. 147–48.

39. Ibid., pp. 131–32.

40. Whitmore, *The Inspirational Life of Robert Sengstacke Abbott*, p. 10, http://www.theabbottinstitute.org/assets/abbott_brucewhitmore_thelifeofrobertsengstackeabbott.pdf; Michaeli, *The Defender: How the Legendary Black Newspaper Changed America*, pp. 49–50, 54.

41. Ottley, *The Lonely Warrior*, pp. 193–94; Rice, *Chicago Defender*, p. 8; Ottley, *The Lonely Warrior*, pp. 208–11.

42. Rice, *Chicago Defender*, p. 8; Ottley, *The Lonely Warrior*, pp. 352, 351; Rumore, "Bud Billiken Parade 2017: If you go," http://www.chicagotribune.com/news/ct-bud-billiken-parade-2017-if-you-go-htmlstory.html; Michaeli, *The Defender: How the Legendary Black Newspaper Changed America*, p. 191.

43. Rumore, "Bud Billiken Parade 2017: If you go," http://www.chicagotribune.com/news/ct-bud-billiken-parade-2017-if-you-go-htmlstory.html; Ottley, *The Lonely Warrior*, p. 352.

44. Michaeli, *The Defender: How the Legendary Black Newspaper Changed America*, p. 145; Motley, *Knock on Any Door*, https://www.goodreads.com/book/show/257127.Knock_On_Any_Door. The ages and order of these two boys, Willard Motley and Robert Watkins, are not consistent in all the sources I have read. It appears that Robert Watkins was the first (at age 10) and that Willard Motley was later. According to a Tribune article, when "Willard was 13 he sent a short story to the Chicago Defender newspaper. The editors were so impressed that they offered him a weekly column, and thus did he become the first of many to write under the byline of Bud Billiken . . ." (http://www.chicagotribune.com/entertainment/ct-remembering-willard-motley-20150402-story.html) According to Michaeli, Watkins was the first editor, picked from among the newsboys selling the paper (*The Defender: How the Legendary Black Newspaper Changed America*, pp. 133–34). Roi Ottley says that Motley (whom he claims was age 10 at the time) was the first Bud Billiken (*The Lonely Warrior: The Life and Times of*

Robert S. Abbott, p. 352). I chose not to say which came first or later, and I also chose the age of Willard Motley as reported by the Tribune (Kogan, "Remembering forgotten writer Willard Motley," *Chicago Tribune*, http://www.chicagotribune.com/ entertainment/ct-remembering-willard-motley-20150402-story.html). There is a photo of the first Bud Billiken in the Rumore article about the parade and the origins of Bud Billiken. The photo is identified as Robert Watkins, and the date is April 2, 1921, when the column was first printed (Rumore, "Bud Billiken Parade 2017: If you go," http://www.chicagotribune.com/news/ct-bud-billiken-parade-2017-if-you-go-htmlstory.html).

45. Michaeli, *The Defender: How the Legendary Black Newspaper Changed America,* p. 133.

46. Rumore, "Bud Billiken Parade 2017: If you go," http://www.chicagotribune.com/news/ct-bud-billiken-parade-2017-if-you-go-htmlstory.html; Michaeli, *The Defender: How the Legendary Black Newspaper Changed America,* p. 145.

47. Rumore, "Bud Billiken Parade 2017: If you go," http://www.chicagotribune.com/news/ct-bud-billiken-parade-2017-if-you-go-htmlstory.html; Michaeli, *The Defender: How the Legendary Black Newspaper Changed America,* pp. 182–83.

48. "Bud Billiken Parade and Picnic," https://en.wikipedia.org/wiki/Bud_Billiken_Parade_and_Picnic; Whitmore, *The Inspirational Life of Robert Sengstacke Abbott*, p. 16, http://www.theabbottinstitute.org/assets/abbott_brucewhitmore_thelifeofrobertsengstackeabbott.pdf.

49. Ottley, *The Lonely Warrior*, pp. 337–38, 220–21, 12, 13.

50. Ibid., pp. 13, 35–36.

51. U.S. Bahá'í Office of Communications, "Encounters with 'Abdu'l-Bahá," "'Abdu'l-Bahá in America, 1912–2012," https://centenary.bahai.us/encounters.

52. "Hull House," Virginia Commonwealth University Libraries Social Welfare History Project, https://socialwelfare.library.vcu.edu/settlement-houses/hull-house/.

53. Moffett, "'Abdu'l-Bahá's Historic Meeting with Jane Adams." *The Bahá'í World*, vol. 6, part 4, p. 682, https://bahai.works/Bahá'%C3%AD_World/Volume_6/Part_4/'Abdu'l-Bahá's_Historic_Meeting_with_Jane_Addams,_by_Ruth_J._Moffett.

54. Abbott, Robert S. "Chicago Defender." May 4, 1912. Available in the U.S. Bahá'í Archives.

55. Whitmore, *The Inspirational Life of Robert Sengstacke Abbott*, p. 9, http://www.

theabbottinstitute.org/assets/abbott_brucewhitmore_
thelifeofrobertsengstackeabbott.pdf; Buck, "The
Baha'i 'Race Amity' Movement and the Black
Intelligentsia in Jim Crow America: Alain Locke and
Robert S. Abbott," p. 18, https://bahai-library.com/
pdf/b/buck_race_amity_movement.pdf.

56. Ottley, *The Lonely Warrior*, pp. 14, 84–85.

57. Buck, "The Baha'i 'Race Amity' Movement and
the Black Intelligentsia in Jim Crow America: Alain
Locke and Robert S. Abbott," p. 19, https://bahai-
library.com/pdf/b/buck_race_amity_movement.pdf.

58. Whitmore, *The Inspirational Life of Robert
Sengstacke Abbott*, p. 15, http://www.
theabbottinstitute.org/assets/abbott_brucewhitmore_
thelifeofrobertsengstackeabbott.pdf.

59. Ottley, *The Lonely Warrior*, p. 362; Whitmore, *The
Inspirational Life of Robert Sengstacke Abbott*, p. 15,
http://www.theabbottinstitute.org/assets/abbott_
brucewhitmore_thelifeofrobertsengstackeabbott.pdf.

60. Ottley, *The Lonely Warrior*, p. 21.

61. Michaeli, *The Defender: How the Legendary Black
Newspaper Changed America*, p. 232.

62. Ibid., p. 234.

Bibliography

American Radioworks. "Remembering Jim Crow." http://americanradioworks.publicradio.org/features/ remembering/transcript.html.

Best, Wallace. "Chicago Defender." Encyclopedia of Chicago. http://www.encyclopedia.chicagohistory.org/ pages/248.html.

Buck, Christopher. "The Baha'i 'Race Amity' Movement and the Black Intelligentsia in Jim Crow America: Alain Locke and Robert S. Abbott." *Bahá'í Studies Review*, Volume 17, 2011. https://bahai-library.com/ pdf/b/buck_race_amity_movement.pdf.

DeSantis, Alan D. "A Forgotten Leader Robert S. Abbott and the Chicago Defender from 1910–1920." Department of Communication, University of Kentucky. Journalism History v23 pp. 63–71, Summer '97. http://questia.com/library/journal/1P3-18533497/a-forgotten-leader-robert-s-abbott-and-the-chicago.

"Founder Editor—Robert S. Abbott." Newspapers: The
    Chicago Defender. http://www.pbs.org/blackpress/
    news_bios/defender.html.

Grossman, Ron. "The Great Migration: For southern
    blacks, Chicago offered jobs—but not the warmest
    welcome from whites." *Chicago Tribune.* April 12,
    2018. http://www.chicagotribune.com/news/opinion/
    commentary/ct-perspec-flash-great-migration-south-
    african-americans-0415-20180410-story.html.

"Hull House." Virginia Commonwealth University
    Libraries Social Welfare History Project. https://
    socialwelfare.library.vcu.edu/settlement-houses/hull-
    house/.

Kogan, Rick. "Remembering forgotten writer Willard
    Motley." *Chicago Tribune.* April 3, 2015. http://www.
    chicagotribune.com/entertainment/ct-remembering-
    willard-motley-20150402-story.html.

Michaeli, Ethan. *The Defender: How the Legendary Black
    Newspaper Changed America.* New York: Houghton
    Mifflin Harcourt, 2016.

Moffett, Ruth J. "'Abdu'l-Bahá's Historic Meeting with
    Jane Adams." *The Bahá'í World,* vol. 6, part 4. https://
    bahai.works/Bahá'%C3%AD_World/Volume_6/
    Part_4/'Abdu'l-Bahá's_Historic_Meeting_with_Jane_
    Addams,_by_Ruth_J._Moffett.

Motley, Willard. *Knock on Any Door.* Northern Illinois University Press, 1989.

Ottley, Roi. *The Lonely Warrior: The Life and Times of Robert S. Abbott.* Chicago: Henry Regnery Company, 1955.

Rice, Myiti Sengstacke. *Chicago Defender.* Charleston, SC: Arcadia Publishing, 2012.

"Robert S. Abbott." NNDB [Notable Names Database]: tracking the entire world. Soylent Communications. http://www.nndb.com/people/733/000141310/.

Rumore, Kori. "Bud Billiken Parade 2017: If you go." August 11, 2017. http://www.chicagotribune.com/news/ct-bud-billiken-parade-2017-if-you-go-htmlstory.html.

Sambol-Tosco, Kimberly. "Historical Overview: Education, Arts, and Culture." Thirteen: Media with Impact. PBS. https://www.thirteen.org/wnet/slavery/experience/education/history.html.

U.S. Bahá'í Office of Communications. 'Abdu'l-Bahá in America, 1912–2012. "Encounters with 'Abdu'l-Bahá." https://centenary.bahai.us/encounters.

Watson, Andrea V. "Chicago's Bud Billiken Parade Celebrates 85 Years." *Chicago Defender.* August 8, 2014. https://chicagodefender.com/2014/08/08/chicagos-bud-billiken-parade-celebrates-85-years/.

Whitaker, Jan. "What Would a Nickel Buy?" *Restaurant-ing Through History.* July 31, 2013. https://restaurant-ingthroughhistory.com/2013/07/31/what-would-a-nickel-buy/.

Whitmore, Bruce W. *The Inspirational Life of Robert Sengstacke Abbott.* July, 2016. http://www.theabbottinstitute.org/assets/abbott_brucewhitmore_thelifeofrobertsengstackeabbott.pdf.

Williams, Mark A. The Willard Motley Collection at NIU. http://libguides.niu.edu/rarebooks/motley 2001.

WTTW, "DuSable to Obama: Chicago's Black Metropolis," p. 1. https://interactive.wttw.com/dusable-to-obama/black-business.

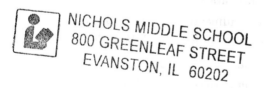